A Sojourner

To Dr. Raymond Bahor,

Love,

Jane Hwa Hu

Jane Hwa Hu

Noble House

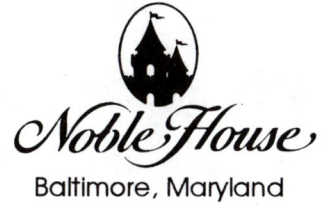

Baltimore, Maryland

A Sojourner

Copyright © 1994 Jane Hwa Hu

All rights reserved under International and Pan-American copyright conventions. No part of this book may be reproduced, stored in a retrieval system, or transmitted in any form, electronic, mechanical, or other means, now known or hereafter invented, without written permission. Address all inquiries to the publisher.

Library of Congress
Cataloging in Publication Data
ISBN 1-56167-145-2

Published by

Noble House

8019 Belair Road, Suite 10
Baltimore, Maryland 21236

Manufactured in the United States of America

With love, I dedicate this book to
my parents, husband, and children.

Introduction

As a publisher of fine poetry, it was destined that Jane Hwa Hu and I would meet. It was through her poetry published here, at the National Library of Poetry, that I first became acquainted with Jane's writing. And with each new encounter, my respect for her skill as a poet grows.

Born in Lanzhou in 1940, Jane remains an active and well-respected poet in her birthland of China. She renders untrue the adage "East is East and West is West and never the twain shall meet" through her skillful blending of the two cultures. And it is in the end — on the written page — that Jane brings a vitality and depth of expression that few poets can match.

If you are new to the works of Jane Hwa Hu, prepare yourself for an enjoyable and thoughtful trip around the world of man and the world of ideas.

> Howard Ely
> Managing Editor
> National Library of Poetry

A POET'S SENSE OF SELF
(for Jane Hwa Hu)

Transplanted from China into the west,
you are an enigma in search of a self.
You think your own thoughts and feel your own feelings.

You write of scent of tea and music, of murmuring
people and scent of tea, of poetry
floating on fragrance in a Ginza teahouse.

You write of, the beauty of loneliness
and holy bliss of existence; you meditate
on self and remember the footprints of friends.

You write of silence in fallen snow
and the hand of God as you walk through your maze
and of the moonlight swims - you are the fish.

You write of our Universe of light and sound
and minicosmologies in atoms and flowers —
inspiration to you beyond understanding.

You are an enigma discovering yourself.

                                              Bruce C. Souders
                                              September 3, 1992

(First published in volume 8, **The Poet's Domain** by the Road Publishers, 1992)

Table of Contents

Introduction	v
A Poet's Sense of Self	vii
A Sojourner	1
To My Readers	2
A Winter of Illness	3
Dream of a Friend	4
The Night of Ocean City	5
The Creator	6
Spruce Lake	7
The Lotus	8
Poetry	9
The Maple	10
Tea House	11
Morning Snow	12
On the Green Meadow	13
Questions	14
In Memory of a Shooting Star	15
January Snow	16
Hometown	17
Me and the Universe	18
Lamps of Souls	19
Consciousness	20
Fascination of Dusk	21
A Repeated Dream	22
Swimming in the Moonlight	23
My Spirit Soaring Free	24
City in the Night	25
Springtime in Washington D.C.	26
Dreams and Reality	27
Count the Days	28
The Poorest Rich Boy	29
The Universe	30

Table of Contents, cont.

Happiness	31
A Wedding Wish	32
Circle of Eternity	33
Life and Death	34
First Love	36
Realizations	37
Havana	38
Karma	39
Mission	40
Free of Passion	41
Pilgrimage	42
My Home	43
Sunset in Kuwait	44
Soul Mate	45
Dreams of a Soul	46
Imminent Thunder	50
Nostalgia	51
Sunrise	52
Memories	53
Lone Ranger	54
June 4, 1989	55
Love	56
Sunset City	57
Moon and Dawn	58
Spring, 1992	59
Terrace Cafe	60
Zen of Tea	61
The Swan	62
Autumn Trees	63
Somalia	64
Bird Nest of Sunset	65
Drifting Souls	66
The Reine River	67

Table of Contents, cont.

Lausanna	68
Mirrors of Hearts	69
Yellow Tropical Fish	70
Jumer Castle Lodge	71
City of Cornfields	72
Sarasota	73
Tomorrow	74
A Pelican	75
Rainy Harbor	76
Nothingness	77
The Yellow River is Calling	78
A Changing World	79
Rome	80
Migratory Birds	81
29 Palms	82
America	83
Home of My Youth	84

A SOJOURNER

I was sent here,
  and came reluctantly.

I forgot who I truly am,
  where I am going,
    what I am supposed to do.

I dreamed that I could fly,
  as free as a bird,
    as bright as an angel.

I was lost,
  a wingless sojourner,
    searching for my way in a world not my own.

In the dark moments of my journey,
  I broke my heart,
    and injured my bones.

With pain in every step,
  I struggled on,
    searching for my way and the light.

Light came to me in deep darkness,
  voices in my dream told me,
    where the destination is.

I know where I am going,
  without the direction how to get there,
    it seems up to me to find it.

The light in my heart is growing,
  brighten my way and those
    who share the lamps of their souls with me.

Now I see the beauty of the world around me,
  the souls of those I love,
    and the happiness of a sojourner who knows.

August 22, 1990

TO MY READERS

Life is a mystery,
   difficult to comprehend,
   impossible to explain,
   only poetry can sketch it with a few lines.

Life experiences pass through me,
   such poignant and illusive feelings,
   joy and ecstasy mixed with tears and sorrows,
   only poetry can express it with simple words.

Poetry can not tell a lie,
   it reveals naked secrets of my heart;
   with such honesty it speaks to those
   who can truly understand.

Touch my feelings with yours,
   poetry is the language of soul.
When your rhythm vibrates with mine,
   suddenly, you seem to know every fiber of my soul.

                                  December 25, 1990

A WINTER OF ILLNESS

A few leafless trees covered with ice,
A blackbird stood alone on top of the chilly branches.
Gently and silently falling,
The snow was as white as fleece.

Roses were all withered,
Under the snow the green grass was buried.
Life, it seemed,
was struggling in the wintry cold.

Underground below the ice and snow,
The roots were still growing.
The rhizomes of tulips were sprouting,
waiting for the sunshine and warm breeze of spring.

It is like the grass in the winter perishing,
Green again in the spring.
The flowers falling and again blooming,
Life is growing continuously without ending.

"The bitter winter is here,
Can spring be very far?"

February 25, 1978

DREAM OF A FRIEND

Last night,
   in a vague and chaotic dream ...
   suddenly, I saw you vividly.
Shining with smiles,
   you seemed to say:
   "Here I am."

Drifting up and down in this world,
   I long forgot about you
   who died so young like a shooting star.
Could it be that the separation between life and death
   was like the misty fog in my dream?
Could it be that you had never left?

The new moon of the pine hills
   remembered your laughters and jubilations.
In the purple dusk of green fields,
   your thoughts and whispers still floated.
I was afraid only the wind in the bamboo trees
   could appreciate our debates.

Only you and me alone
   could understand with smiles in the fog of a dream...

                                             August 13, 1978

THE NIGHT OF OCEAN CITY

Passing by this night city near the ocean,
   on the remote lonely beach,
   we walked slowly along the gulf of the sea.

Waves after waves,
   the passions of ocean subsided in tranquility.

The tides retreated,
   and rose again,
   following the rhythm of the ocean in eternity.

The night had no moon and no stars,
   only the endless mystery and darkness.

We sat on the sandy hill side by side,
   like a pair of dim lamps,
   facing the eternal challenge of time and ocean.

The unchanged among the million changes
   is the unperishable truth.

We turned around;
   there were myriads of lights in the city,
   a delusion of this brief life.

We smiled,
   hand in hand, following the sea breeze,
   walking back to dreams and delusions.

                                  August 16, 1978

THE CREATOR

On top of the cliffs of Africa,
   hundreds of apes faced the east.
They stared motionlessly;
   they waited silently.

The first beam of dawn,
   light overcame the darkness.
The apes waved their arms making noises with happiness,
   joy overwhelmed in their vague consciousness.

Same as millions of living creatures,
   the Ancient Egyptian Emperors and Queens,
   the travellers and camels in the ageless deserts,
   all witnessed the arrival of dawn with solemn awes.

It was the first beam of Holy Light and Spirit,
   like the light of dawn in early morning,
   chased away the darkness of ignorance,
   brought to the world the glory of humanity.

Green spring grass is hope;
   summer flowers are myriads of smiles;
   storm is anger.

A beam of white light in the forest,
   it is the sublimation of love,
   the purification of fire.

Human life is an inspiration,
   a sigh of compassion.

Almighty holy spirit and thoughts
   are silent prayers of pure hearts.

He is in everything;
   He is everything.

                                August 17, 1978

SPRUCE LAKE

The silver green spruce trees,
  in the fog and clouds,
  embraced the jade blue lakes.

The Grand Mesa of Rocky Mountains,
  layers and levels of spruce trees,
  high and low were hundreds of lakes.
Extending endlessly in the distance
  were misty mountains.

Tonight, we camped by the lake shore,
  burning the campfires —
    the flames sparkling,
    the pine scents refreshing...

Silently, we listened to the wind in the woods —
  the bird singing,
  the tree murmuring...

In the middle of the lake,
  a full moon was shining,
  and myriads of stars twinkling...

Such a beautiful night,
  we could linger along the lake hand in hand,
  or ride horses in the woods side by side.

In silence,
  everything was said.

Only your soft singing and whistling,
  strings of horseshoes pounding,
  broke the silence in the serenity of mountains
  and the reflections of trees in the lakes...

                    August 19, 1978

THE LOTUS

Gently touching the violin strings.
   I let the small boat drifting after the water lilies.
In the sky, the stars blinked,
   shining on the moon in the waves.

The dragonfly was fluttering its transparent wings;
   pearls of dew gleaming on the lotus leaves.

Standing by the moon-shaped bridge,
   could it be she as we first met?
   her white skirt floating in the wind,
   a small round silk fan for the fireflies in her hand...

In the noises of my haste rowing,
   the water drops splashing,
   on the green round leaves they were falling.

In the bright moonlight,
   there was only a white lotus above the waves,
   dancing in the gentle wind,
   standing gracefully with its delicate scent.

                                    August 21, 1978

POETRY

Poetry is a spirit with wings,
    the transparent wings of a dragonfly,
    fluttering in the shadows of flowers,
    spreading a trail of golden powder,
    ringing a string of silvery bells.

It flies through the forest and across the wildness,
    allowing twilight to penetrate the morning fog,
    sunshine drawing circles in the tree leaves.
It follows gentle breeze and white clouds,
    floating toward the infinite azure sky.

Poetry is whispering in the singing mountain stream,
    in the endless blue ocean,
    it opens its arms;
    the waves are murmuring,
    the rushing tides are calling.

Poetry is the inspiration of the spirit,
    the flames of life,
    the sudden flash of the brilliance of humanity.

It follows you,
    watching the disappearance of every dusk,
    waiting for the arrival of a new tomorrow.
When new moon arises,
    setting sun has not faded;
    there is a moment,
    poetry is swinging in the tender wind.

                                  August, 1978

THE MAPLE

In the forest of autumn,
   I walked on the ground covered with leaves.
Red maple leaves,
   like falling flowers
     dancing, swirling, landing and perishing...

I picked up a piece of tender blushing
   with the splendor of sunsetting.
Reflecting against the azure sky and white clouds,
   the autumn crimson dusk covered all the mountains.

It was the life of a leave,
   before its departure from this world,
   burning with all its love.

                                October, 1978

TEA HOUSE

The moon was pale,
   The lights in the Ginza were dazzling.

A transient sojourner,
   Under a lamplight alone,
   Let the smoke and mist drift in the air.

Opening a writing paper on the table,
   I had no need for bitter wine,
   Only the fragrance of tea.

Several volumes of poetry,
   And one pen
   Accompanied me around the world.

                          Ginza, Tokyo

(First appeared in Vol. 8, **The Poet's Domain** by the Road Publishers, 1992)

MORNING SNOW

The dawn of first snow,
  outside the window,
    was a world of shining crystals.

There was no sound in the tranquility,
  only the drifting of snow.

Morning twilight sparkling in the crystalline jade trees,
  wind blew away a forest of silvery flowers.

Who took a silent walk
  in the solitude of the wintry morning?

A row of clear boot prints
  on the spotless ground covered with white snow.

The longer he walked,
  the farther he went,
    the deeper his boot prints...

                              January, 1980

ON THE GREEN MEADOW

Listening to the whispers of the clear stream,
I lay down on the green meadow.
Giant trees and green shades surrounded me
Like a cathedral with a transparent dome.

Through the layers of green leaves,
I saw the bright sky as an infinity of blue,
With circles of threads of while clouds.

The yellow butterflies came fluttering their wings;
The bald eagles circled around.
There were spots of sunlight,
Countless leaves green as jade.

Lying beside the singing stream on a green meadow,
This was a time to rest,
Looking up to the light of the sky and tomorrow.

Suffering was over,
The hot summer at its end,
The coolness of autumn had to be near.

August 18, 1980

QUESTIONS

In the evening rain,
   I wandered around and searching...

The tall palm trees on the campus were the same,
   I returned home and could not find my house any more.

In the bookstore,
   unexpectedly I saw you
   a silhouette on the book cover,
   staring at the ocean, sky and eternity...

Your poetry
   seemed to whisper to me alone.
Dreams and sadness buried more than twenty years,
   why did you unfasten the string of ringing bells in that rainy night?

Outside the window,
   there were chilly wind and tear drops of rains;
   I heard the nightingales crying.

I opened the door of my heart for you,
   wishing you would accompany me in my heart.

I knew that you had never left;
   could you tell me
   how to chase away the misty fog between the living
   and the dead?

Tonight, I sojourned across the ocean,
   could you tell me, where were you?

                                May 10, 1981

IN MEMORY OF A SHOOTING STAR

Endless summer rains
   brought the feeling of autumn;
   they cooled my heart,
   and shadowed my eyebrows with melancholy.

The misty smoke saturated with green
   drifted outside the window, in the woods.

Then, you silently stroke a fiber of my heart,
   played the music of how many memories...

Ah, continuous and everlasting ups and downs,
   life, like gleaming waves and lights,
   danced on the eternal and infinite ocean of Time.

Did you know?
   Your waves had long disappeared from this world,
   you should have followed the tides and returned to the other shore.

Why were you still wandering, lost and trembling?
   On my waves,
   your smiles were still streaming and streaming...

August 7, 1981

JANUARY SNOW

The sky full of white fleece drifting,
   blossoms of snow flowers were falling.

Layers and layers of distant mountains light smoke,
   the foggy wildness was misty as water painting.

The white birch trees covered with crystals,
   snow fell from the shoulders of the green pines.

The earth, silent without a word,
   let the ice and snow decorate a forest of silvery trees and flowers.

January 4, 1982
Potomac, Maryland

HOMETOWN

When I finally see you again,
  Sisters' Ditch at the valley of mountains, my birth place,
  all those happy family members of my childhood
  would have perished and disappeared.
Only this traveller covered with dust coming from thousand miles away
  stand there alone.

I would tell you how much I have missed you,
  Pier Shu by the West Lake with misty waves and
  mountain shadows.
The handsome youth walking on your green grasses in the past,
  his hair had turned grey and already perished prematurely.
Only those willows turning tender green every spring,
  they are probably still the same.

At dawn, I shall come with the twilight,
  when the long night is ended.
The morning sun rises from the horizon of the ocean,
  shining on this great land of mountains and rivers,
  bringing light to billions of you and me.

                                        January 4, 1982

ME AND THE UNIVERSE

You told me to live for today,
   let me tell you,
   I live in every moment.

Breathe deeply,
   life is a delight.

My heart is tranquil with no waves;
   following the swaying of the tree top,
   white smoke floats in the woods like mist;
   the universe and me are in harmony.

I am only consciousness and love;
   the world is a reflection in my eyes.

If I can hear all the waves,
   if I can see all the colors,
   if my consciousness is not such a narrow line,
   could I understand the truth, my universe?

Perhaps, I would know whether it could be truly as I imagine,
   I am a wave in your eternal vibrations,
   a point in your infinite consciousness.

                                    January 12, 1982

LAMPS OF SOULS

In those days I loved to ride my bike,
   following the gleaming waves of the River,
   chasing the setting sun every evening to the Bridge Yin.

I watched the dusk darkening,
   the evening stars rising,
   lamplights reflecting on the waves of the River.

The dusk of summer was violet - rosy as a dream;
   the breath of the evening breeze was intoxicating,
   sweet as wine in the blood of my youth.

I am still a lover of dusk and evening stars;
   on the top of the highest tower of every metropolitan city,
   sitting alone by the window,
   watching the myriads of lights.

An ocean of lamps twinkling like diamonds,
   in the darkness of unknown,
   so sparkle the lamps of our souls -
      encountering, comforting and perishing...

Where is your lamp,
   searching for dawn in the night of this long dream?
I shake away all the dust from my journey,
   shine my dim lamp on you.

Friend,
   I am here.

                              January 7, 1982

CONSCIOUSNESS

The drifting snow and fleece in March
   covered the foot prints of travellers and birds.
The lone crane had gone,
   leaving not a single trace.

Beside the small pond in the Southern country,
   water lilies and orchids were your friends.
Watching the floating leaves drifting together and apart,
   did you feel the affinity of two souls parted in the gentle rain?
Like the candlelight floating on the water
   drifted close to the white lotus blooming in the moonlight.

Tonight, in the silence of falling snow,
   the ocean waves arise and subside in my chest.
When the dazzling colors of this world disappear in the night,
   what exists in my meditation,
   is always myself alone:
      a pure and clear consciousness,
      an everlasting burning lamp of love.

                                      March, 1984

FASCINATION OF DUSK

Dusk had descended,
   the azure sky reflected in the blue lake.
The dark ink of the distant mountains and deep forests,
   with the shadows of clouds and water grasses,
     dyed and penetrated the gleaming water and mountain colors.

My spirit was lingering in the water waves and fading sun,
   like the floating mist above the waves,
     attached to the mountain forests and the green lake,
     longing to catch the last touch of purple dusk in the sky.

The dusk was poignantly beautiful
   like the fading passion.
The desire of youth was quietly disappearing
   in the tranquility of the night...

Suddenly, the new moon appeared,
   the silvery Nature was eternal beauty
   reflecting the everlasting love in human souls.

                                       October, 1985

A REPEATED DREAM

I wander in the colorful woods;
   with love, sunset caresses all trees.
Autumn colors weaving poetry on the strings of my heart,
   memories are so vivid in my pensive thought.

The leaves turn red in autumn,
   the blue sky seems always the same.
Time perishes like leaves falling;
   as the blue sky, consciousness is everlasting.

In every springtime of your life,
   I shall come back to you alive;
   when the first crocus
   appears under the melting thin ice.

Flowers perish and flowers blossom,
   sunrise and sunset, life is a repeated dream.

                                 November 12, 1986

SWIMMING IN THE MOONLIGHT

The sky was full of stars,
   palm leaves waving in the evening breeze.
I was a fish playing in the pond,
   under the moonlight in the gleaming waves,
   enjoying the coolness of the water alone.

In the tranquil silence of the night,
   I moved in the water gently,
   hearing only my breathing.
Like a silvery fish in the seaweeds,
   I played my games with no sound.

The evening breeze was tender as a sigh
   from the feelings of my heart.
Life was a joy of existence,
         a consciousness.

In the sobriety of my consciousness,
   the world, like the shadows of a delusion,
   was fading away and perishing.

In the sober solitude,
   this moment,
   life was perfect, harmonious and lively.
The joy of pure existence
   was wholesome,
   innocent as the smiles of the twinkling stars in the sky.

I floated on the surface of the pond,
   quietly enjoying the sweet tranquility of Nature.
The sea breeze bringing the sound of the ocean,
   the breath and scent of wild flowers,
   the water was never so tender...

                           April, 1986
                           Sarasota, Florida

MY SPIRIT SOARING FREE

God created life to be free,
I can straighten my wings and soar free,
Like the sea gull raising its chest of gleaming feather,
Facing the orange sunset with no fear for thunder.

Human bondages are desires,
Freedom lost in selfishness.
In God's Will are love and creativity,
Without selfishness is liberty.

Following His Will,
One Can steer Destiny.
Love lights the lamp in my soul,
Shining for ever in eternity.

My spirit carries the sea breeze and rainbow dust,
Soaring in the sky and gone with the sunset.

                                        Fall, 1987

CITY IN THE NIGHT

A sparkling city in the night,
Lamps gleamed like dew drops on spider webs.
The village was a few lights far apart in the mist,
Shining with the tranquility of wintry stars.

A myriad of lights blinking in the city,
Were they the same as our souls?
We met in the unknown destiny,
Sharing the warmth and lights in our hearts.

Human souls seeking happiness in ordeals,
Wandering and lost in disillusions.
How much sadness, ecstasy, separations and reunions,
In the life process of birth, aging, death and sickness.

We searched in vain the meaning of living,
Only love in our hearts with hope is always glowing.

>   December, 1987
>   in Northwest Flight

SPRINGTIME OF WASHINGTON D.C.

When the gentle breeze blew through the trees,
Morning mist drifting in the woods;
Cherry blossoms were falling like rain,
Or snow flakes in the season of tender green.

The white flowers were dogwoods,
The deep pink dots, wild cherry blossoms.
Sunlight shone on Lincoln, in his temple of white marbles,
Watching the Mirror Lake with reflections.

The Philosopher's eyes stared at the round top of the Capitol,
Saddened by the sufferings of this world and its ordeal.
The Great Man broke the iron chains of slaves,
Could not untie the bondages in human spirits.

The cherry blossoms were falling like rain,
The spring breeze came again.

April 4, 1989

DREAMS AND REALITY

Maybe life, and everything in life are vanity,
Only our souls and love are truly reality-
　In the misty memories of joy and beauty,
　Of countless springs and youths of eternity.

In a dream of my vivid memory,
There was a moon-shaped bridge of yesterday.
Could you and I stand on that bridge of yesterday,
And share a moment of today?

In my wish and daydreams,
There was a mountain cabin in the snow and pine trees.
Could there be a chance,
You and I would share a moment by the fireplace.

Sharing the peace of souls silently knowing and loving,
Lives are only dreams vaguely passing...

　　　　　　　　　　　　　　　July 3, 1989

COUNT THE DAYS

Give up true feelings and friendship at heart,
One may die young as one's fate,
Like so many of my friends so perfect,
They died young without a fault.

Maybe stupidity is necessary in living,
Passion keeps the flame burning.
Everyday in life we are carefully walking,
As if on ice we are stepping.

How many days you can see my face,
Before life fades away like dreams?
Count the days with your fingers,
And cherish every smile you catch in my eyes.

Feeling is such a rare thing,
In life we have to learn cherishing.

July 14, 1989

THE POOREST RICH BOY

Once you told me,
   your two brothers died of loneliness.
With all the money and no love,
   they drink themselves to death.

There you were,
   lying on the beach drinking alone.
The ocean seemed to whisper music,
   the white sand was soft and tender...

Seeking around in the world,
   where to find something money couldn't buy?
A soul you could touch,
   a heart you could feel...

                                     June, 1990

THE UNIVERSE

In the deep blue space,
Myriads of stars glowed like lanterns.
Covered by ozone and misty clouds,
The earth is a beautiful planet of blue oceans
and green lands.

As the scientist knows,
Only a narrow light spectrum is visible to our eyes,
Only a limited band of sound waves can be
detected by our ears
Is our world truly as we perceive it?

What would our universe and everything truly be
If we could perceive all the light, sounds and waves?
Would non-believers become believers,
And the past, present and future be really continuous?

In an atom,
All the particles orbiting like stars in a universe.
A flower with all its colors, fragrances and vibrations
Is a world by itself.

The light and waves of the universe,
I can sense you only as inspirations,
The unheard songs and whispers
you touch my heart as love and feelings.

HAPPINESS

As a dreamer seeking in his dreams,
   we are searching in our floating lives
   for something which can fill our hearts with joys.

Sitting near a fountain surrounded by autumn flowers and busy shoppers,
   quietly I enjoyed a cup of tea and a moment of peace,
   the tranquility of a peaceful heart filled with bliss.

The fireworks of brilliant colors,
   outside the window of the View Lounge with music and songs,
   happiness is sharing a candle and a sweet marriage with smiles.

It is happiness when you give a toy to a child,
   share your food with the homeless and disabled,
   and help an old lady across the street with your hand.

The beauty of Nature: ocean, mountains, moon and stars,
   the spring flowers and autumn leaves, magnificent sunsets and sunrises,
   even the snow can inspire happiness if you appreciate a moment of silence.

Happiness is in simple things and daily working,
   no money can buy the peace and happy feeling,
   knowing that you have done your best after a day of striving.

Life and death, war and peace,
   trust your fate to God's will and Justice,
   in your heart will always be peace and happiness.

At sunrise, the early morning sky is all rosy,
   the past mistakes, regrets and sadness are dead with yesterday;
   rejoice, we are given another chance and reborn with today!

                               August 16, 1990

A WEDDING WISH

On your wedding day,
  I wish the church bell rings,
    filling the blue sky with divine melodies.

The altar will be decorated with white flowers,
  as pure white as your satin gown with pearls,
    your floating veil, lacy gloves and white roses in your hands.

I wish you will say your wedding vows as a woman
  knowing all the duties of raising a family as a guardian,
    with the support and love of a mature and responsible man.

You and your chosen one will be together always,
  despite all the illness, misfortunes and differences,
    sharing a life of hard working, joys and fulfillments.

Marriage is meant to be
  a promise of life-long companionship,
    a devotion to the family and loving relationship.

The wedding bell rings a blessing
  to a couple sharing the ordeals and rewards of fate,
    building for children of their love a safe nest.

Marriage is willingly giving up
  one's self-centered freedom and indulgence
    for the foundation of a home and future generations.

I wish your wedding vows are solemnly made
  at the right time and place
    with the right person of your mutual choice.

There is nothing more beautiful
  than a silver-haired couple dancing together,
    lovingly sharing the candlelight with tenderness and laughter.

                              To my daughter, Diane
                              August 21, 1990

CIRCLE OF ETERNITY

In my dreams,
  it seems
    there is a bridge
      across the past, future and forever...

I found myself in Rome of the past,
  dancing in my barefoot,
    hearing my father's roaring laughters,
      seeing him vividly as an Italian gentleman with curly hairs.

Crossing a bridge in ancient Japan,
  I dressed in silk kimono and gold embroidered coat,
    sight-seeing in a city after sunset in the purple mist
      the lamps glowing in the flowing river like strings of pearls.

In a long white robe with veil in Saudi Arabia,
  in my dream I was chosen to serve as Royal official;
    it has to be sometime in the far future-
      when women can serve as officials in that desert country.

Oh, I dreamed of China of tomorrow,
  people celebrated the victory of a democratic election;
    the hallway of the executive building shining with white plastic,
      I murmured to myself, This has to be changed to white marble.

What is past and future?
  They seem to exist at the present;
    as an endless circle,
      we travel in our lives and dreams.

Where did our past disappeared to?
  Where is our future waiting for us?
    I only can touch them in my dream --
      bridge across the past, future and eternity...

                              August 22, 1990

LIFE AND DEATH

As a dreamer seeking for his dreams in a dream,
   we are searching for happiness and success in our lives.

Maybe, only after death,
   we shall wake up from a dream,
   everything in the world is vanity of vanities
   only the growth of souls and love is everlasting and continuous.

Maybe, only after death,
   we realize that life is truly a dream,
   a play with written scripts,
   an experiment repeated again and again for learning.

Maybe, only after death,
   we clearly understand the total picture of our lives:
   where we have gained knowledge and growth,
   when are the times we have lost our way and failed.

What are really valuable in life
   and what are empty and meaningless.
True feelings are engraved in our souls;
   fame, wealth and glories are gone with the wind.

People who live their lives in the light,
   shall find the brilliant light at the end of the tunnel.
Those who spend their days in darkness,
   shall face the shadows of their evils.

The peonies perish in the winter,
   its rhizomes under the ground covered by snow
   are waiting for the sunshine of next spring
   to bring new sprouts of another season of blossoms.

Human souls are rhizomes of lives:
   they sprout new forms in the spring of every generation.
Death is the end of life;
   death is also the beginning of another life.

Life follows death,
   and death follows life,
   generation after generation,
   the cycle of nature continues in eternity.

                              August 22, 1990

FIRST LOVE

It was so long ago,
   when everything faded with time,
   I could still see you leaning against the white marble column,
   smiling at me like a prince from my dreams.

You took me home in a carriage,
   rain drops pouring in from the window,
   such joy overwhelming to find each other,
   sweet rain drops flowing from your face to mine with smiles.

In a classroom,
   near the window,
   under the moonlight,
   we shared the innocent moment of tenderness.

Never again,
   love can be so pure,
   divine without desires,
   passion without lust as the first love.

Walking in the dark streets hand in hand;
   running along the river in the misty yellow dusk;
   sharing warm toasted chestnuts in a movie;
   such poignant happiness would never repeat in life.

I have travelled endless miles,
   I have met countless faces.
Still, I often wonder where you are,
   are you well and are you happy?

You were the first one
   touched my soul and entered my heart.
I will always remember you,
   as I remember the carefree young girl of my youth.

                                        August 23, 1990

REALIZATIONS

"The fear of God
   is the beginning of knowledge."
Every lie is punished;
   all good deeds are rewarded.

We wonder why the innocent suffers
   and the evil spirits succeed?
Only because we can not perceive
   the complete Justice after each one's death.

The world is an idea,
   reflections of His image everywhere,
   power of his will,
   creation of his love.

His kindness is in the morning light;
   His inspirations in the budding flowers.
In dreams He gives me instructions;
   subtly He blocks my turns to temptations.

I am only the clay in His hands,
   how could I question my master:
"When is my time ready?
   How are you going to shape my destiny?"

I have done my best
   and continue to strive everyday.
Quietly I try to enjoy my daily toil,
   preparing and waiting for His tender calling.

                         December 16, 1990
                         Boston

HAVANA

Paris of Caribbeans,
  with all its glamor, charm and follies,
  sparkled like a cubic diamond with myriads of lights.

The dancing girls were beautiful and seductive,
  the gamblers intense and cool,
  the rich insatiably indulging and the poor desperately suffering.

In the eve of revolution,
  the city seemed bustlingly alive,
  dancing with flames and exotic Caribbean drum beats.

Behind the alluring shadows of dancers and songs,
  there were gunfires and blood,
  fightings in the dark streets and falling bodies...

Like fireworks magnificent and brilliant in the sky,
  silvery soap bubbles shining with rainbow colors,
  Havana of yesterday was a city of dreams at sunset.

In the twilight of fading dusk,
  true love was found more valuable than diamonds,
  human nobility a torch burning in the darkness.

Life is just such a colorful and poignant dream,
  it will eventually disappear in vanity,
  only love and noble spirit shine through eternity.

December 25, 1990

KARMA

Sitting across the Japanese table,
    you arched your shoulders like the ancient samurai in my dream.
Years accumulated grey hairs and wisdom,
    age added maturity and serenity.
Time seasoned feelings and friendship
    as mellowed and fragrant as the warm saki.

As a young girl walking in the street long ago,
    I turned my head and saw your eyes sparkling with surprise.
What in me attracted you for life,
    I would never know.
It was wonderful for you and me
    to sublime a tragic attraction to friendship warm and pure.

We toasted a sip of saki,
    joking about what might have happened in ancient Japan.
Why did you follow me like a shadow for years
    and I hated you with such a passion?
Could it be that you had to pay for
    what you did in the long forgotten past?

Thirty years passed in a blink,
    Taipei became a city I could not recognize.
Gone were the youthful you waiting in the street
    and me in the black skirt and green blouse.
Gone were the unexplainable passion and hatred,
    the days of aimless searching and drifting.

We toasted our friendship and understanding
    no one else in the world could share.
You found yourself,
    and I have my destination.
With such sincere friendship of souls,
    we probably would meet again in another life and place.

                                      January 3, 1991

MISSION

Push every inch I could,
   while I am awake.
Clean my thoughts,
   watch every step I take.
Catch every square inch of opportunity
   God made it appearing in front of me.
I do not know what else I could do,
   but pray for his guidance.

Make all the efforts I could,
   I know God holds the key.
Committing no sins,
   I shall not fall.
Find enjoyment in my daily toil,
   I can eat, sleep and rest in peace.

God's mission is always possible,
   He knows my capacity.
He has given me His orders,
   everything should be in His plan.
Follow His Will with faith and earnesty,
   I shall live to accomplish His words and mission.

                              January 16, 1991

FREE OF PASSION

I have to tell you, my friend,
   I came to this cafe alone
   to visit the table we shared.

Thinking of you with the same pure heart,
   my friendship flows like mountain stream:
   cool, clear and for ever. . .

I am a pilgrim, my friend,
   on my long Journey I have to be free of passion,
   a burden a pilgrim has to let go.

I think of you with the same smiles:
   such richness in your thoughts,
   I wish I could explore.

Let go of your burdens, my friend,
   we might have a chance to meet again,
   sharing the warmth and understanding of glowing souls.

I have to tell you, my friend,
   I cherish a heart of solid gold,
   there are not many souls as pure as yours.

Sitting alone in this cafe,
   I am wondering how you are,
   wishing you a Happy New Year and peace in heart.

                                        January 20, 1991

PILGRIMAGE

Life is a pilgrimage with a purpose,
  an ordeal to purify our souls.

As a pilgrim,
  I travel my lonely roads.
With courage and will,
  I shall prevail.

In silence I gain strength;
  with knowledge I see wisdom.
I surrender my life to you,
  my God and Humanity.

Let go forever,
  my personal gains and losses.

There is light and infinity,
  bright and shining in the mind of selflessness.
My consciousness is totally free,
  vibrating with love and rhythm of the Universe.

                        January 31, 1991

MY HOME

Thirty years in a place I call my home,
   weaving golden dreams in those youthful days,
   cultivating my children with smiles and tears,
   toiling and striving in this land of opportunities.

Too many unfair events I do not want to recall,
   miseries and sufferings are simply part of life.
It is sad to realize after those long years,
   I am still a stranger in my home.

In this life I am really a sojourner on earth,
   my eternal home is where Love and Light reigns.
Living only to accomplish my mission,
   I have learned to let go my personal gains, losses and feelings...

Life is a dream, a pilgrim and a mission;
   my eyes and heart are set on my destiny.
Opening my arms and sharing my love with all people and places,
   my home in this world is truly everywhere and any place.

                                                February 21, 1991

SUNSET IN KUWAIT

The setting sun was sliced by drifting clouds,
   flattened and distorted by smoke and fog.
The sun, top and bottom parts, was misty orange and vague
   the middle section was pinkish, slightly out of place.

The deep blue sky was tinted by purple color,
   night arose as dark shadows from the desert.
It was uneasily quiet,
   soldiers hiding in the darkness for another night of relentless war.

The pointed tops of Moslem temples,
   with their single and double circular domes,
   pieced the colorful sunset with their dark presence,
   on the silent sand casting mysterious shadows.

Suddenly, fire bursted in the oil fields,
   flames reaching the sky and stars.
Black smoke and explosions filled the air,
   the purple dusk disappeared in a devilish red glare.

This world was and still is an eternal battle
   between the good and the evil,
   between the light and the darkness,
   between life and death forever and ever in process...

                                        February 28, 1991

SOUL MATE

All we need in life
   are a few souls sharing our joys and pains.
How many have we met
   who could truly feel our souls?

Someone who could touch my heart
   and sense my thoughts.
Someone who could understand my ideals
   and struggle with me to achieve life's missions.

Drinking a cup of tea by the fountain,
   I wonder who could enjoy with me such simple delights in life?
Always chasing the sunsets and sunrises since my youth,
   could there be another soul who could understand?

Drifting in life with my fate,
   could I meet smiling eyes seeing through me knowingly?
Searching for my destiny in the foggy Unknown,
   could some hands hold me up when I stumble?

Knowing my mission and destination,
   without the knowledge how to achieve it,
   I know God has planned helping friends.
   Could there be a soul mate to travel with me the lonely roads?

In the candle light, a few silvery hairs shining,
   My husband and I celebrating Mother's Day alone.
With gentle eyes and half of a smile,
   he seemed to say, " I am always here with you!"

                              December 13, 1990
                              Revised May 13, 1991

DREAMS OF A SOUL

1.

Lying on the ground in front of the Emperor,
   I lowered my head in fear.
I had no clothes on and naked like many others,
   my body was covered with self-afflicted healing scars.

The Emperor ordered me to raise my head,
   in my dream, I was very surprised.
His eyes sparkled as we first met this lifetime,
   could he really be an Emperor in the Ancient time?

The Ancient Emperor was known to prefer doing nothing,
   it might be possible to be a professor and enjoy golfing.
What an amazing stone age dream and the simple palace,
   how vivid were his sparkling eyes and the primitive scenes.

2.

I dreamed of the white marble palace along the Nile River,
   the moon was silvery and the water was crystal clear...
The majestic column casted long shadows in the moonlight,
   the marble stairways leading gracefully into the water.

Forced to marry my scheming pursuer,
   I decided to swim away along the river.
"Catch the Queen or kill her!," yelled the person I did recognize,
   My body was pushed into the river by the servants.

A silver hunting folk gleaming in the water,
   I struck the servants and killed the evil pursuer.
The Nile River flowing with crimson color,
   I quietly walked into the water...

3.

In a brief dream vivid as a picture,
   I dressed as a young warrior with short hair.
Sitting on the grass in boots, hunting pants and a dark green shirt,
   I shared the campfire with my Lieutenant.

The sky was dark with a few stars,
   the night was tranquil with chilly breeze.
He offered me a bottle of red wine and cheese,
   and a woolen blanket to spend the night in the wilderness.

Bundled under the warm blanket,
   my comrade was beaming with delight.
He discovered me as an innocent girl with blush,
   the surprises and feelings somehow still fresh...

4.

Crossing a moon-shaped bridge in a time ancient,
   I dressed in a silk kimono with a gold chrysanthemum coat.
The river was slowly flowing,
   in the misty dusk the street lamps were glowing...

A young samurai with a straw hat on his shoulder,
   he stood in front of the station next to the river.
We exchanged a glance with such mixed feeling,
   next to him, I saw a pretty girl standing.

His face was so clear and vivid,
   who could he be? I wondered.
Twenty years later I recognized that person,
   someone I avoided since my youth with a passion.

5.

My father was an Italian gentleman with curly hair,
   he laughed roaringly with joy and flair.
Our house was full of guests,
   what a plentiful feast with wild games and fruits.

Surrounded by young men and admiring eyes,
   I danced in floating long skirt without shoes.
How confident I was,
   all their hearts belonged to me and no one else.

I climbed the stairs to avoid the crowd,
   on the roof, alone I walked.
The evening air was intoxicating with flower and pine scent,
   the wind was fragrant and free as my spirit!

6.

Dressed in satin gowns and pearls,
   Ylanda and I were sisters sitting in a magnificent opera house.
Clapping our hands together as a game to play,
   we were excited and happy.

Overlooking the blue ocean and rocks,
   our beach house had a white marble patio with columns.
I dressed in a white gown with shoulder straps,
   my long brown hair and beauty stunned the dreaming me and others.

Along the long beach of white sand.
   I rode a white horse following my loving husband.
The sky was blue and clear,
   the ocean was timelessly tender and azure...

7.

At dawn, drifting in our backyard woods was morning mist,
   orange blossoms were golden and fragrant.
I washed my face with cool fountain sprinkles
   the dogwood outside the window covered with white flowers.

Warm and cozy was our small brick house,
   on my writing desk was a vase full of dainty daisies.
In the kitchen, baking chocolate cakes,
   smilingly I watched two daughters with golden curls licking the bowls.

Wearing a white dress with long skirt and tiny black dots,
   I cheerfully greeted my husband walking into our house.
Smiling broadly with a healthy glow and long wavy hair,
   my husband carried a wooden tool box of a carpenter.

8.

The China of tomorrow,
   billions of people cast their votes.
Thousands of happy faces in a huge Hall,
   with joy and tears they celebrated the victory.

Victory of democracy and freedom,
   people's Will chose their leaders and future.
I walked down the hallway with white plastic walls and murmured:
   "This has to be changed to white marble for this great country!"

It is a dream of the future,
   it is also a vision shared by millions today.
If it is written somewhere in the circle of eternity,
   we shall wait patiently for that day to come.

May 13, 1991

IMMINENT THUNDER

The setting sun was orange and round
  with a yellow glow in the desert sand.
The pointed tops of Moslem temples with circular domes,
  In the misty amber dusk cast long shadows.

The new moon was faint as a silvery eyebrow;
  the immense desert was dark and silently the wind blew.
In the Persian Gulf the high tides rose,
  rushing to the sandy beach with splashing waves.

In the darkness of the desert sand,
  soldiers crawled forward without a sound.
Riding on the high tides,
  landing boats arrived quietly on the ocean shores.

Stealth airplanes soared in the sky like eagles,
  tanks moving across the desert in countless numbers.
Dark shadows on the sea were carriers and warships,
  hiding behind the sandy camouflage, myriads of soldiers.

Suddenly, there were thunders,
  lightnings in the sky without stars.
Cannons, bombs and missiles,
  explosions and fires lit up the darkness.

With anguish and frightening cries,
  shadows of cities and people collapsing in the chaos.
The fires of war and oil fields burned the sky crimson red,
  until the final silence, the imminent thunders roared...

                              June 25, 1991

NOSTALGIA

Dreams of lives,
   like white lily onion skins,
   wrapped around my soul layer after layers,
   I saw myself appearing, overlapping in the semi-transparent dreams.

I dreamed of the Nile River,
   moonlight glittering in the clear water.
The moon-shaped bridge in ancient Japan with street lamps
   reflected in the river like strings of pearls...

The Opera House in Paris,
   the banquet in Rome,
   the great country of Yellow River and the simple palace,
   with such nostalgia I saw them in my dreams.

Going through the trials of my life,
   I stood up heroically and I fell in pieces;
   I cried with heart-broken sorrows, I laughed with such delights,
   now I am pensive.

All the pleasures in life are no longer alluring,
   I feel no need for anything more than simple living.
If I do not have my life's duties,
   I would rather disappear with the wind into the clouds.

SUNRISE

The sea gulls flying from the lonely rocks to the water:
   the misty sky and ocean were one silvery color.
Suddenly a golden thread appeared beyond the horizon,
   with brilliant light the morning sun rose above the ocean.

Sea breeze blowing on my hair,
   my white skirt floated in the air.
I heard the ocean's calling and whispers,
   summer wind caressing my face with such tenderness.

The ocean tide rose and fell in harmony,
   against the rocks the waves splashing.
The ever-changing sea had unchanged beauty,
   in the sunlight the azure water glittering.

Welcome you, my rising sun,
   another morning and another to-day.
Tomorrow was still hiding somewhere unknown,
   disappeared forever in the darkness of last night was yesterday.

What a beautiful morning,
   you made me forget and forgive this miserable world.
Pulsing with the waves were my heart and blood,
   just to be alive and breathing was such a blessing.

                                            July 11, 1991

MEMORIES

"Mommy, when I grow up,
 can I marry you? "
"No, Darling, I would be too old,
 you will marry a young and pretty girl."
"But I think you are the prettiest,
 you look just like a Barbie doll."
I hugged my son,
 knowing how much he loved me.

We walked in a street covered by yellow autumn leaves;
 I carried him across the street in my arms.
"Mommy, please do not move away,
 I want to visit you whenever I can."
I embraced my son and held his head against my heart,
 the pain was still there with my swallowed tears.
Fate had forced us apart, tearing us in pieces,
 Merciful God reunited us and healing us with love.

It is a pilgrimage to strengthen our bodies and souls,
 I visit my son whenever I can.
There is no need to say anything,
 just to watch him, touch him and kiss him on the cheek.
A brilliant and young lawyer,
 there is a part of him will mature and heal only in mother's love.
Together we restore the bridge to the long lost past,
 together we walk toward a future bright and full of joy...

July 29, 1991

LONE RANGER

Sitting on a rock in the pine woods,
   I listened to the song of wind through the pine trees.
Watching the purple dusk disappearing behind the mountain,
   I felt the lingering love of the setting sun.

I long to talk to someone
   who could share my feeling and burden;
   someone who could see beyond my physical presence
   into the depth of my soul and essence.

When I struggle to find my destiny,
   I am alone seeking for the guidance of stars.
Life is a transient and lonely journey,
   floating on the tides of our fates.

No one, including me, could comprehend
   what could be my modest role in this world?
It could be rare to find some souls
   who would appreciate my dreams and poems.

I am here,
   facing the world and my fate as a lone rancher;
   wandering in my dream searching for God's instruction,
   writing poetry in the woods alone...

                                            September 10, 1991

JUNE 4, 1989

The Chinese students stood facing the army tanks fearlessly,
   refusing to give up their dream of freedom and democracy.
They spread their arms, chests and pounding hearts,
   let the tanks crush their bodies under the rolling wheels...

"Without freedom,
   I would rather die!"
Reaffirming the human spirit for equality and freedom,
   young blood flew at Tienanmen under the blue sky.

On June 4, 1989, the martyrs died.
   under the mother earth, like seeds dead and buried.
From them Peaceful revolution as spring grass widely spread,
   from Eastern Europe to Soviet Union, communism collapsed.

The movement of freedom and democracy rose like a giant tide,
   riding on the time and following the natural trend.
The Will of all people
   now faces the massive challenge of the Great Wall.

The movement started in China
   shall end in China.
When China is free,
   the world will be free.

                                           September 11, 1991

LOVE

Life is only the instrument of love.
   Love creates life,
   and provides the source of energy for life.

Love inspires,
   it motivates,
   and sustains life.

In life,
   we are constantly driven,
   tirelessly striving,
   endlessly seeking,
     in search of love.

There are love of souls,
   love of beauty,
   love of humanity and the world.

Love is divine inspiration,
   seeking for pleasures and greed is not love,
   searching for love is longing for God.

                        September 30, 1991

SUNSET CITY

Here I came again, all alone,
   watching the crimson sunset and violet dusk
   disappearing into the dark blue ocean...

Myriads of summer flowers vanished in the wintry wind,
   the ocean still murmuring gently,
   I missed the autumn sunshine glittering like gold.

The patio facing the ocean and waves
   still full of the fragrance of blossoms,
   it seemed so empty without the patio umbrellas and golden smiles.

I sat next to the fireplace
   feeling the warmth of the dancing flames:
   these small things and memories touched my heart and its strings.

As a sojourner, coming and going,
   the images of cities and people appearing as layers of dreams,
   I had learned to sigh silently and shed my nostalgia and feeling.

                              December 7, 1991

MOON AND DAWN

Daylight perished with the setting sun;
   on the pine top appeared the new moon.
This world and its follies all faded,
   only the moon and tranquility in my solitude.

The misty yellow wilderness at dusk I remembered,
   how I was lost in the spring of youth.
The mist of innocence and ignorance finally dissipated,
   I could clearly see an endless path.

Destiny still hiding mysteriously,
   I would wait quietly;
   waiting for the end of the long night,
   till the twilight of dawn revealing my way to the East.

Flying with the wind and twilight,
   I would come with the morning sunlight.

                                          March 24, 1992

SPRING, 1992

Looking out of my window,
   I suddenly noticed the touch of green in the leafless trees.
Still no sign of life on the tall branches of willow,
   tender green already spread like mist in the woods.

Across the street in the Kenwood Place,
   cherry blossoms were glorious ocean of clouds.
Lavender, purple and white crocus
   nodding cheerfully with the yellow daffodils.

The bitter winter was finally ending,
   Spring brought hope and new beginning.
If one dared to take destiny in one's hand,
   dreams were possible as God promised.

My heart was touched and my spirit strengthened,
   how God's Will worked in miracles.
Before we could imagine our need,
   He had long prepared for our battles.

Embracing my mother's picture with love and gratitude,
   I seemed to see her joyful tears.
Because of her gift unexpected,
   I could be ready for my life's struggles.

                                        April 10, 1992

TERRACE CAFE

I came here, a nest on the terrace,
   like a bird flying to its favorite tree.
Enjoying the wild flowers in the vase,
   with peace, I drank a cup of perfect tea.

Sitting next to the window,
   overlooking the delicate leaves of green woods.
Silvery rain and afternoon sun wove a faint rainbow
   casting its glory on the buildings and museums.

Like my lunch plate of bread and fruits,
   the joy of life could be so easy.
Listening to the summer rain dripping on the leaves,
   on the napkin, I wrote a poetry.

From God, Life is a gift;
   happiness is made of simple things and a pure heart.

                   June 5, 1992
                   East Wing,
                   National Museum of Arts
                   Washington, D. C.

ZEN OF TEA

Always in the gentle music and sound,
   candlelight tenderly gleamed.
In a tranquil and dim corner,
   I meditated with scent of tea and people's murmur.

My spirit was far away from the noisy world
   entering 'into a wilderness with leaves green as jade.
My spirit lingered like mist in the woods of bamboo trees,
   my heart, following the breeze and flower scents,..

In a brief lifetime, brilliant or mediocre
   success and failure;
   everything is vanity of vanities,
   vanishing eventually into wind and clouds.

How much stupidity could there be in this world,
   human cruelties, battles and sufferings never ceased.
One could easily let go of his burdens,
   this empty life's ecstasies and agonies.

Only this moment,
   revelation in a blink is transparent.
The existence is holy bliss.
   With tea scent and melodies...

                                          July 14, 1991
                                          Taipei

THE SWAN

I was so young yet so sad,
   as if half of my life was crushed dead.
Recovering from agony, weak and fragile,
   I spent most time in a rocking chair facing an empty wall.

Playing an old record again and again,
   I listened to the slow and graceful rhythm of The Swan.
As swans moving gracefully on the lake in the moonlight,
   the warm and tender cello soothed my broken heart.

The sweet music of the violins
   vibrated in my soul and echoing with silent songs.
In an empty room and the tender Swan melody,
   I found consolation and serenity.

Life could be such sufferings,
   God gave me strength and blessings.

                                               July 28, 1992

AUTUMN TREES

How the trees in the woods
Revealed their true identities in the autumn mist.
They stood there in such tranquility and elegance,
With brilliant colors fading and characters always last.

All the trees looked the same in the summer greens,
In autumn, suddenly they became totally different.
The maples were tender and passionate full of crimson leaves,
The leafless birch pensive and the green pines still vibrant.

The graceful trees stood on the soft meadows,
Nature's beauties, poets and philosophers in the morning mist.
Touching the sky and God with their delicate fingers,
Life's peace and love was found in a tree's silent heart.

I watched the trees everyday from my window,
Their spirits I seemed to finally recognize and know.

October 29, 1992
Bethesda, Maryland

SOMALIA

Through Baidoa the American troops escorted food
   the tough marines wept and the starving Somalis smiled.
Children with sticky legs and potbellies,
   they greeted the army of liberation with smiles.

The marines were trained to kill with no fear,
   now they faced the duty to feed and care.
As His instrument of love and grace,
   God chose the most powerful armies.

Why did countries fight meaningless battle?
   Why did people kill their own and other people?
Famine could wipe out generations,
   human greed and cruelties would eliminate the whole race.

Why was there so much stupidity we would never know,
   God called the United States to restore hope for tomorrow.

                                        December 17, 1992
                                        Bethesda, Maryland

BIRD NEST OF SUNSET

A small L-shaped apartment,
   on the sixteenth floor overlooking the Hudson River,
   wall to wall windows framed the magnificent sunset,
   purple mist drifting above the flowing water...

Everything in the room glittered in gold and crimson,
   a bird nest transformed into a palace by the magic moment.
   A struggling student with a toddler son,
   I felt rich as a queen facing the sunset.

When the moon casted its silver light into the river,
   our oval lamp reflected its soft glow on the window.
   Bygone memories warmed my heart forever,
   a cozy nest with carpet as green as meadow.

By the lamp I studied into midnight,
   my darling son lying in bed insisted to wait.

                                   To my son, John
                                   December 18, 1992
                                   Bethesda, Maryland

DRIFTING SOULS

I walked on the ancient, rocking stairways,
   trying to avoid the piled up antiques.
In a room of a different country among the strangers,
   in my dream, we were lonely sojourners.

We looked at each other in the eyes,
   communicating without a word.
The depths and sensitivities of Chinese souls,
   only we could silently understand.

As if, only in dreams,
   I realized we were still drifting souls,
   strangers in a different world,
   the hindrance of things people owned.

What is solid?
   In this life what is permanent?
   Isn't our brick house in Maryland?
   The nights are tranquil and lamps are soft.

Is it Taipei city
   where we grew up under the Palm trees?
   Unfortunately, wealth and prosperity
   have diluted human feelings.

Could it be my hometown
   where I was born?
   The Yellow River came from the mountain in the cloud,
   the immense plain covered with yellow sand.

Are you not contented with golden dreams?
   Oh, drifting souls!

                                  July 25, 1992

THE REINE RIVER

In the summer night of Bonn, under the bridges,
   the Reine River was quietly flowing.
Across the River, like myriads of diamonds,
   street lamps were glowing.

The brilliant lights dancing in the river
   decorated many cities of power and glamor.
In the tranquility of Holland
   to the free ocean the Reine joyfully returned.

How many wars with their glories and agonies
   the river had silently witnessed?
Like the flowers of bygone springs,
   the great Emperors came and perished.

Only the Reine River was still quietly flowing
   from yesterday to tomorrow never ending...

                                August 13, 1992
                                Bonn, Germany

LAUSANNA

Amber dusk,
   peachy clouds,
   dark green Alps embraced the blue Lake,
   purple sheen of sunset glittering in the water and the Alps.

On the patio of red flowers and green pines,
   yellow lamplights glowing in the dusk;
I sat there quietly watching the white birds
   lost myself to the mountain and the lake...

Summer night arrived as mist rising from the lake,
   dark shadows falling from the Alps.
Along the curved shore of the lake,
   a myriad of lights sparkle on the slopes of the Alps.

Music and songs came from Lausanne,
   a mirage at sunset with magic and beauties.
Lausanne, a city of charms from the lake to the mountain,
   seemed a dream dazzling with lights and melodies...

We rowed a small boat
   gliding on the lake and tranquility.
In the misty night,
   Lausanne, it was pure poetry.

Sitting at a table of the street cafe,
   we toasted a glass of wine in the moonlight.
Transient as dew and dream was our life,
   I gave you a red rose tonight!

                        August 17, 1992
                        Le Lacustre Restaurant
                        Lausanne

MIRRORS OF HEARTS

Let go of personal gains and losses,
   nothing can disturb inner peace and happiness.
Happiness is to use one's potentials
   to do one's best for others.

Happiness is to know that one has done the best;
   selflessness is the fountain of inner peace.
Our conscience is the temple of our spirit,
   a clean conscience is a holy place.

If our conscience is clear as mirrors,
   we see our past, future and present.
Shine and clean our conscience,
   we may see God's idea and thought.

The beauty of the world,
   life's wonders and joys,
   the power and love of God,
   all are revealed in the mirrors of our hearts.

                          December 23, 1992
                          Bethesda, Maryland

YELLOW TROPICAL FISH

I woke up smiling last night,
  such a delightful dream,
    like joy singing in my heart.

I dreamed of my daughter Diane,
  a princess yellow tropical fish,
    swimming happily in the emerald blue ocean.

There were deep pink spots above her eyes,
  such poignantly beautiful colors,
    glowing like a pair of rubies.

The dream probably had no meaning,
  only my heart was full of love and delight
    grateful for God's blessing.

        To my daughter in Okinawa, Japan
        for her birthday
        February 2, 1993

JUMER CASTLE LODGE

Sitting by the fireplace,
   with my body and soul in one piece,
   I remember with thoughts pensive,
   the trauma of the past a dream illusive.

Twenty-five years have passed,
   my broken spirit is now pure and solid.
The crying little boy is now a man successful,
   God's love is healing and wonderful.

Vividly I could see myself walking in the rain,
   carrying a red umbrella covering my beloved son.
Time has disappeared unknowingly,
   life seems to slip by inevitably.

Sitting in the patio cafe facing the Mall,
   overlooking the half-empty hall,
   I shall continue to live and love peacefully,
   though the world has changed drastically.

                            March 17, 1993
                            Lincoln Square
                            Urbana, Illinois

CITY OF CORNFIELDS

The light and soft snow was falling,
  a grey sky full of clouds darkening.
The taxicab drove by the city covered with snow and ice,
  passing strange streets with names evoking poignant memories...

Students' dormitories standing there in the snow and mist,
  in a world of mountains of snow and frost,
I seemed to see a microbus in the blizzard,
  and the golden smile of a little boy with parents reunited.

On this campus surrounded by cornfields,
  the dream of a small family was broken apart.
Looking back in this tranquil town and streets,
  I saw clearly how fate ripped apart my life and my heart.

It seemed I came here to reconcile with years bygone,
  passing by the old places of sad memories.
Thinking of the success and happiness of my children,
  now I could face the past with nostalgia and peace.

New generation had grown strong and beautiful,
  it came my time to enjoy life and be grateful.

March 19, 1993
Urbana, Illinois

SARASOTA

By the window facing the evening bay,
   I sat at the Boathouse Cafe staring at the gleaming water.
Many, many years disappeared like yesterday,
   I used to come as a bird flying to the South every year.

It would be satisfactory as my life's goal,
   protecting the scientists' endeavors like an angel.
Fate assigned me a different path,
   I left without a word and nothing to soothe.

Still caring for people I had not met on this land,
   never again I could be so deeply attached.
Maybe in my hometown on the other continent,
   millions of people are waiting for hope that fills my heart.

Sarasota, I came back once again in the evening,
   spring flowers were still blooming.
The white sand, blue ocean and twinkling stars,
   all appeared unchanged in a town full of memories.

I, somehow, seemed to be a total stranger,
   lost in the noises of people's chattering and laughter...

                      April 13, 1993
                      The Hyatt House
                      Sarasota, Florida

TOMORROW

Every day a new beginning,
  one works hard today,
  tomorrow will be worth waiting.

Our future we do not know,
  one dreams and strives,
  waiting for tomorrow.

Tomorrow, finally one breaks all the bondages,
  able to use one's full potentials,
  shining as light and flying to the stars...

April 14, 1993
Sarasota, Florida

A PELICAN

On a post in the bay,
   a pelican slept comfortably.
Its long beak on its chest,
   the eyes were closed for a tranquil rest.

With cool ocean breeze,
   the sailboats rocked with blue waves.
Spring sunshine warm as mother's caress,
   the pelican was in perfect harmony with the universe.

The scents of wild flowers
   following the waving leaves of green palms,
   I found in my soul,
   the ever present peace was eternal.

In life, why are we constantly seeking?
God's gift is this wonder of living.

                            April 14, 1983
                            Boathouse Cafe
                            Sarasota, Florida

RAINY HARBOR

Thunders in the distance,
   sea birds flying over the waves,
   misty dusk fell with rain drops.

How quiet was the rainy harbor,
   deserted by the crowd,
   only silvery rain silently falling into the water.

Wild daisies seemed smiling,
   oh, the peace of existence and life,
   with Joys the palm leaves dancing.

Watching the rain with serenity,
   sensing the world as reflections of my consciousness,
   I felt my heartbeats and breathing in tranquility.

                                 April 15, 1993
                                 Sarasota, Florida

NOTHINGNESS

Nothingness,
    except the essence of life and soul,
    everything is nothingness.

In life there seems so much anguish and sorrows,
    and such joy and ecstasy in love and power,
    they all vanish as the dream ends.

Death is awakening;
    success and failure, losses and gains,
    only shadows in dreams we chase.

A dreamer seeking for his dreams,
    until he finds peace in his purified soul,
    life is but a dream of vanities.

                                April 15, 1993
                                Sarasota, Florida

THE YELLOW RIVER IS CALLING

I revisited places I had lived,
   with my past I made peace.
Touring the cities I have loved,
   I bid farewell to Venice.

It's time to go home,
   I could feel a river flowing in my soul.
Being a sojourner for so long drifting in a dream,
   now I have to search for my life's goal.

Maybe it's the place I was born,
   from the sky the Yellow River passing the mountain,
   flowing through the endless land of yellow sand,
   where I might find a vision billions of people have shared.

It's time to go home visiting,
   the Yellow River is calling.

May 14, 1993
Rome, Italy

A CHANGING WORLD

There seemed to be hope for peace
   after endless suffering of war.
Today Israel and the Palestinians signed for peace,
   could a new era begin with a brighter future?

Could an enemy become a friendly neighbor?
   the changing world transformed like clouds.
From a jungle of cruelty and atrocious war,
   might this world someday become a land of peace?

It all happened like dreams in a few years,
   since young Chinese students were crushed at Tienanmen.
Millions stood in the streets in Eastern European countries,
   democracy was won through peaceful revolution.

Soviet Union was declared dead;
   like a phoenix arising from the ashes,
   the giant in the North again revived,
   suffering and changing in the ordeals of reforms.

How unbelievably fast the Germans were reunited;
   by human hands the Berlin Wall was torn down.
Could the Chinese someday be reunified
   and drifting souls go home to their hometown?

Like dreams so many things happened
   in a few years of this changing world.

                               September 13, 1993

ROME

The Colosseum at sunset,
   the grandeur of the ancient ruin seemed eternal
   still lingering in the air, the anguish of the warrior spirit
   facing a meaningless struggle with a savage animal.

Surrounded by flowers, I walked up the Spanish Steps,
   marveled at the splendid water fountains.
In the spring of my youth, Rome seemed a city of flowers,
   Elegant Romans had endless time for leisures.

I revisited Rome thirty years later,
   the magnificent marble wonders still there.
What a depressing difference time had made,
   was I aged or Rome changed?

Motor cycles and people rushing in the streets,
   elegance and leisure were as rare as roses.
Grand mansions and marble statues were abandoned,
   though every stone in Rome like antique should be cherished.

Sunset again at the Colosseum,
   grey mist and yellow dust covered the brick roofs.
The moon in Rome was always the same,
   eternally beautiful as the ancient ruins.

                                          December 12, 1993
                                          Taipei, Taiwan

MIGRATORY BIRDS

Every winter,
  I returned to this Pacific Island.
Like migratory birds,
  I went home to the warm South.

Welcome come,
  migratory birds,
  the Island greeted me with prosperity;
  Taipei was crowded and bustling with traffic.

What happened to the rice fields and tranquility?
  the quiet streets and peaceful lamps in Taipei?
  the sounds of wooden slippers in the silent alleys?
  the flute music of the blind offering messages at night?

My home in the green shadows of palms,
  and the memories of my youth,
  the era of innocence and hope,
  all were buried under the skyscrapers.

I could no longer smell the lotus and bamboo trees,
  Taipei, I had so deeply attached,
  so stubbornly holding on with my soul,
  had vanished and let go of my sentiments.

Yet, I still came back,
  like a migratory bird,
  searching for a home vanished,
  feeling lonely in my hometown as a stranger.

                              December 22, 1993
                              Taipei

29 PALMS

In the desert with no trees,
  only the barren plains and sandy hills,
  it was the training ground for desert war,
  testing the strength of soldiers and weapon power.

With helmet, vest and water bottles,
  I climbed into the transport helicopters,
  almost blown away by the wind,
  and choked by the sand.

I could swear,
  the marines tried hard to hold back their laughter.
It was quite an experience
  for this group of women in all sizes, colors and shapes.

Following the desert warfare step by step,
  walking up and down the sandy hills nonstop,
  some women even pulled the cannon triggers,
  with thunders and fire, the smoke darkened the clouds.

War was not meant for every woman,
  we were convinced by this visit with a purposeful plan.
If little old ladies could pass this test,
  could one doubt that some women might have warrior spirit?

> October 19, 1993
> Fall Conference of DACOWITS
> (Defense Advisory Committee on
> Women In The Services)
> Palm Springs, California

Note: After the Fall Conference of DACOWITS, Secretary of Defense Les Aspin opened up many opportunities of army and marine positions which previously excluded women.

AMERICA

The majestic Rocky Mountains,
   the Grand Canyons and sunset in the desert are magnificent.
America is still a dreamland of great potentials,
   in the blue mountain lake, one can always catch rainbow trout.

Why are the dream seekers from the world crowded in the cities,
   seeking golden dreams in the dark street alley?
The inner cities of America are seized by crimes and poverty,
   turning dreams into disillusions and miseries.

Hard work and determination can break all barriers,
   one can be free to shape one's destiny.
In America, there are always opportunities,
   if one is willing to strive with honesty.

America, America, hope of the world,
   you are the symbol of democracy and freedom,
  devils' battlefield and playground,
   home of good people and God's Kingdom.

                                          December 6, 1993

HOME OF MY YOUTH

In the warm spring breeze,
   the willow flowers drifted like snow flakes.
How I could still feel the impulses of that long lost spring,
   my heart pounding with the sunshine and willow flowers drifting.

Outside the green silk screen window,
   the blue sky was tender and mellow.
Sitting at my old desk,
   I could hardly focus on my book.

In my mother's small round mirror,
   I took a peek at myself with wonder.
Mother sitting next to a window,
   with a fine tweezer, smilingly she trimmed my eyebrow.

How well I remembered our Japanese styled house,
   Father reading newspapers in a rattan sofa next to the
   blooming orchids,
  Mother watering pink orleanders in the garden,
   in the wind all those I cherished were gone...

The home of my youth and memories,
    memories of those innocent days and loved ones,
   all vanished like dreams under the ground,
    under a highrise building the home of my youth forever buried.

                                       December 6, 1993